How to Sail

An Introduction to Sailing for Beginners

By: Karl A. Minner

Acknowledgement

Getting a book written, proofed and published is no small job. I want to thank the many people that were instrumental in bringing this idea to life. In particular, I would like to thank friends and family for helping me with the selection, editing and proofreading of this book.

Table of Contents:

Introduction

Sailing is fun.

Sailing is a timeless pursuit, sport and recreation that is steeped in tradition, but yet remains on the cutting edge of physics and technology.

When you enter the world of sailing your very orientation to the world changes. Not only do you have to learn the language of sailing you have to learn just what makes a boat tick.

Unlike powerboats that run on gasoline and row boats that are powered by physical strength, the actual power plant for a sailboat is its sails that utilize the wind to propel it forward.

This book was written as a practical guide that is designed to get you involved in learning the basics of sailing with a basic keel boat. In particular, you will learn how a sailboat works, some common commands and sailing terminology and everything in between.

Whether you have never been sailing or would like to know enough to be helpful on your friend's boat or plan to get your own boat this book has something for you. Use it as a tool building for launching your exploration into sailing.

In short, once you have read this book you should be familiar with:

- **how to leave a mooring;**

- **how to return to a mooring;**

- **how to make a sailboat go where you want it to go;**

- **how to identify the points of sail;**

- **how to adjust the sails to use the wind;**

- **and much more.**

That said, I want to take to moment to **Welcome you Aboard!**

Now, let's get started.

Chapter 1:
Know the Common Sailing Terms

Sailing is a unique sport and recreation that is steeped in tradition and dates back over 5000 years. As you add to your sailing vocabulary, you are going to find that some of the terms make perfect sense, while others may seem a bit arbitrary.

Aside from the terms used for the different parts of the boat, there are also certain terms that sailors commonly use while at sea or heading out. Some of these are:

- **Port**: When you are facing the bow (the front of the boat) the side to your left is the port side.

- **Starboard**: Starboard is the right side of the boat when facing the bow.

- **Windward**: As the name might imply, windward is the direction the from which the wind is blowing, upwind.

- **Leeward**: This is also called 'Lee'. This is the direction to which the wind is blowing, downwind.

- **Tacking**: Tacking is when you turn the bow of the boat through the wind so that the wind switches from one side of the boat to the other. This is when you most need to be mindful of the boom, as the boom will swing from one side of the boat to the other when you tack (you don't want to be in its way when it does that.)

- **Jibing**: This is the opposite of tacking, which means that it is when you turn the stern (or back) of the boat through the wind so that wind shifts to the other side of the boat. This is a more dangerous maneuver in a

3

strong breeze than tacking since the boat's sails are always fully powered by the wind, and may react violently to the change in the orientation of the boat to the wind. Care must be exercised to control the boom during this maneuver as serious injury is a possibility if the boom travels across the cockpit uncontrolled.

- **Trim**: To pull the sails in.

- **Ease**: To let out the sails.

- **Luffing**: This is when the sails begin to flap and lose drive caused by steering the boat into wind or easing (loosening or over-easing) sheets.

- **Starboard Tack**: wind is coming from the starboard (right) side of the boat.

- **Port Tack**: wind is coming from the port (left) side of the boat.

Chapter 2:
How Does It Go?

The Principle Behind Sailing: the Bernoulli Effect

If you've never thought about it, you might assume the wind always moves a sailboat by pushing it. This is true when a sailboat moves in the same direction as the wind. The wind fills up the sail and pushes the boat along. Running with the wind can be especially exciting when flying the big, bright spinnaker sail.

How is a sailboat capable of moving in any other direction other than being pushed by the wind? Answer: the wind pulls the boat. The principle is the same as the one that makes airplanes fly and allows sailboats to sail 45 degrees into the wind. It is called the Bernoulli Effect.

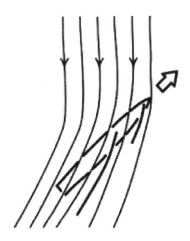

Close hauled

Two things are required to make the Bernoulli Effect take place: moving air (or fluid) and a surface curved on one side.

When air moves over the curve (such as the rising curve of an airplane wing or the outward curve of the sail), that air moves faster than the air moving underneath the curve. This creates lower pressure on the top of the wing or the outside of the sail. This difference in pressure creates lift for the airplane and sailboat. The lift on the boat is what creates the pulling effect.

Because of this effect one of the sailor's main jobs is to keep the curve of the sail correct. Sailors call this "trimming the sails." Sailors adjust the trim by pulling in on or releasing the sheet secured to the clew of the sail. When the sail is correctly trimmed, it stays taut and works efficiently to move the boat. If it is not trimmed correctly, it luffs and spills wind. The boat does not move efficiently.

Chapter 3:
Know Your Sailboats

If you are a beginning sailor you will most likely not be operating your own schooner. You will probably be working with a catboat, cutter, or sloop. That said, it is helpful to be able to identify sailboat types which are denoted by number and location of masts on the boat. The six types are:

- sloop,

- cutter,

- catboat 'cat',

- ketch,

- yawl,

- schooner.

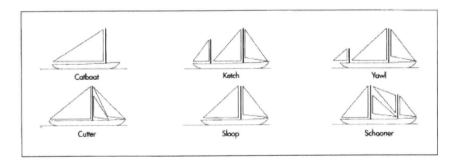

Sloop:

When we picture sailboats, these are normally what come to mind. Sloops are the most common type of sailboat. It has a single mast and is rigged up with a jib in the front and a mainsail attached to back of the mast. They can range in size and are ideal for sailing upwind. If they have just two sails — a foresail and a mainsail — then they are referred to as a Bermudan sloop, said to be the purest type of sailboat.

Cutter:

Cutters have one mast with two sails in the front and a mainsail on the back of the mast. These boats are meant for small crews or groups of people and can be handled relatively easily.

Catboat 'cat':

A Catboat has a mast set up near the front of the boat and is a single-sail boat. They are small (or large, for that matter) and easily operated by one or two people.

Ketch

A ketch is a two-masted sailboat, a main mast forward and a shorter mizzen mast aft. But not all two-masted sailboats are ketches — they might be yawls. In other words, the mizzen is shorter than the mainmast and is in front of the rudder.

Yawl

Yawls are similar to ketches with the difference being that their mizzen masts are located behind the rudder. The reason for this placement is that the mizzen on yawls is for keeping balance, rather than for moving the boat forward.

Schooner

The schooner while totally unpractical has a romantic charm. Such a yacht features two masts of which the foremost is shorter than the mizzen (opposite of a ketch rig). Schooners are large sailboats with two or more masts. The mast in the back of the boat is either taller or equal in height to the mast at the front of the ship. Schooners have been used to commercially fish, transport goods and as warships.

Chapter 4:
Parts of a Sailboat

The common sailboat comprises eight essential parts: hull, tiller, rudder, mainsail, mast, boom, jib and keel. The hull is the shell of the boat, which contains all the internal components. Its symmetrical shape balances the sailboat and reduces drag, or the backward pull caused by friction, as it moves in the water. Inside of the hull in the stern, or back of the boat, is the tiller, which is attached to the rudder in the water. Think of the tiller as the boat's steering wheel and the rudder as the tire. To maneuver a sailboat to the right, for example, you pull the tiller to the right side of the boat, causing the rudder to alter its direction.

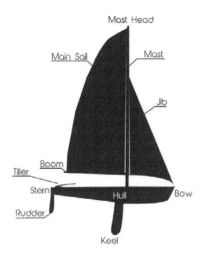

If you think of the tiller as the steering wheel, then the sails and the keel are the engines. The mainsail is the larger sail that captures the bulk of the wind power necessary to propel the sailboat. Its vertical side attaches to the mast, a long upright pole, and its horizontal side secures to the boom, a long pole parallel to the deck. Sailors can rotate the boom 360 degrees horizontally from the mast to allow the mainsail to harness as much wind as possible. When they pivot the boom perpendicular to the wind, the mainsail puffs outward.

Conversely, it goes slack when swung parallel to the wind. This freedom of movement allows sailors to catch the wind at whatever angle it blows. The jib is the smaller, fixed triangular sail that adds additional power for the mainsail. The keel, a long, slim plank that juts out from the bottom of the hull, provides an underwater balancing force that keeps the boat from tipping over. In smaller sailboats, a centerboard or daggerboard serves the same purpose as the keel, but can be raised or lowered into the water to allow for shallow water sailing.

Shipboard Directions:

I thought it necessary to quickly identify shipboard directions, in case you ever find yourself on a friends boat or yacht. In general, you'll want to remember that the bow is the front of the boat and the stern is the back. The forward is the area moving towards the bow and the aft is the area moving towards the stern.

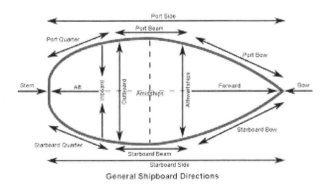

General Shipboard Directions

What's more, anything on the left side of a boat is the port side of the boat and anything on the right is said to be on the starboard side.

Chapter 5:
Sails and Rigging

In sailing there are two typical kinds of sail: the mainsail and a smaller foresail or jib.

The mainsail is the big sail behind the mast and is obviously very important to how the boat works. The mainsail is controlled by a single mainsheet that usually runs to a series of pulleys in the middle of the cockpit. The pulleys supply the extra force need to move the big mainsail when it is full of wind.

The top corner is called the The top corner is called the head, the bottom corners are the clew and the tack. On this sail, the tack is close to the mast and the clew is at the end of the boom. The sides are called the foot at the bottom, the luff at the front near the mast and the diagonal leech at the back.

Parts of a yacht and rigging

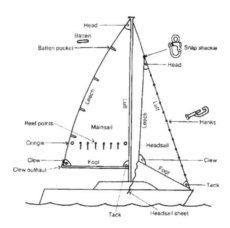

The jib is equally important to how a boat sails, especially when it sails into the wind. As you can see from the diagram the naming conventions are the same, but there is no attachment of the sail to a boom a on the mainsail.

The jib is controlled by two sheets which run down each side of the boat. When the boat is sailing one of these, the working sheet, will be under load as it holds the force of the wind in the sail. The other, the lazy sheet, will be lying slack – essentially doing nothing. When the boat changes direction the lazy sheet and the working sheet will swap sides. The lazy sheet will hold the sail against the force of the wind and become the working sheet and the working sheet will go slack and become the lazy sheet.

Rigging is the ropes and wires on a boat involved with sails. Every 'rope' is named for its function and/or location. This is so when the skipper says "dump the mainsheet and take in the jib!" everyone knows which rope to let go and which one to pull. A topping lift is used to raise or lower a spar, like the boom. A halyard raises or lowers a sail and would thus be attached to the head of the sail. A sheet is a rope that controls the angle of the sail to the wind. It is usually attached to the clew.

Mast- The vertical spar from which the sails are set

Forestay- Rigging extending from the bow to the front of the mast

Spreaders- Struts extending from the sides of the mast which keep it from bending sideways

Jib- The forward sail which attaches to the forestay

Shrouds- Rigging wires extending up the sides of the boat to the mast which keep the mast from falling to either side

Traveler- The track that controls the sideways (athwartships) movement of the boom

Mainsheet- The line running between the traveller and the boom used to control the mainsail

Boom- The horizontal spar extending back from the mast. The foot of the mainsail is attached to it

Batten- A slat of fiberglass, plastic, or wood inserted into a pocket in the sail to help hold its shape

Backstay- Rigging extending from the top of the mast to the stern

Mainsail- The sail hoisted on the back side of the mast and attached to the boom

In addition the sailor should know about the coomon hardware on a sailboat. There various pieces are winches, shackles and cleats:

Winches:

The forces involved in sailing are sometimes more than a single human can handle. To help we use winches. A winch is a mechanical device which multiplies the force you can put on a rope. Because of the forces involved, winches can be dangerous. You should keep your fingers clear of ropes on winches if you don't want to lose them!

Shackles:

A key shackle secures one line (e.g., the main halyard) to a part in the rigging (e.g., the main sail). The key in the pin locks into place, making a more secure connection.

A snap shackle secures one line (e.g., the spinnaker halyard) to a part on the rigging (e.g., the spinnaker). The bullet is spring loaded. To open, pull the ring back. The bullet will spring back into place when the ring is released

A hook shackle secures one line (e.g., a pole topping lift) to a part on the rigging (e.g., spinnaker pole). closure is spring loaded. To open, push the closure in. It will spring back into place when released.

A horn cleat holds a line by means of specific knot, i.e., a cleat hitch. To secure the line, tie a cleat hitch. To release, untie the cleat hitch.

Cleats:

A clam cleat holds a line between two sets of scalloped teeth. To secure a line, push the line down into the cleat. To release, pull the line while lifting it straight up

A cam cleat holds a line between two spring loaded jaws. To secure a line with a cam cleat, pull the line through the cleat while pulling it down between the jaws. To release, lift straight up

A jam cleat holds a line by pinching it into the narrow part of an inverted "V". To secure a line , jam the line up into the inverted "V". To release, pull the line down out of the "V".

Chapter 6:
Putting Up and Down Sails

One job you'll have to do a lot is putting up a sail or taking it down.

Normally a sail will be fastened to itself or the boom with sail ties to stop it flopping around. These must be removed before anything else happens. Be careful in strong wind as the sail might catch the wind and fly around.

It might also be necessary to attach the halyard or the sheets to the various corners of the sail. A halyard is normally attached with a shackle, a kind of steel pin. When moving a halyard you must hang on to it at all times – if you let it go, it might slip up the mast and someone will have to go and fetch it!

On a jib, a sheet is normally tied on with a knot called a bowline. On a main, the mainsheet is normally permanently attached to the boom or attached with shackles.

Once the halyards and sheets are attached and any sail ties have been removed, the sail may be raised by pulling on the halyard.

Mainsails are heavy. Normally one person stands at the mast and sweats the halyard – they take a big handfuls of rope and haul the sail up – while another person takes in the slack on a winch.

Once a sail is raised as far as it will go by hand it will probably have to be winched the rest of the way. It is good practice to keep the halyard on a winch as you raise it, then you only need to insert a winch handle and crank it the rest of the way up.

To raise the mainsail :

- Remove any sail ties

- Attach the halyard and sheet if necessary

- Put the main halyard on a winch

- Open any jammers which might be securing the main halyard

- Turn the boat into the wind (this will keep the wind out of the sail while you raise it)

- While one person sweats the halyard another takes in the slack on the winch

- When the sail won't go any further, insert a winch handle and crank it up until its taught

- Cleat, lock off or otherwise secure the halyard

To lower the mainsail:

- Put the main halyard on a winch, take up the tension

- Turn the boat into the wind (this will keep the wind out of the sail while you lower it)

- Tighten the mainsheet so the boom doesn't flap around and give someone concussion

- Undo any jammers which might be securing the main halyard

- Ease out the halyard

- When it is safe to do so someone can move up onto the cabin roof and gather up the sail against the boom as it falls. When it has been gathered up sail ties can be tied around it.

Furling sails

Some boats (especially of the charter variety) have a special type of sail called a furling sail. This is most often found on jibs but can be found on mainsails as well. A furling sail wraps itself around a stay or around/inside the mast.

For example a furling jib will wrap itself around the forestay. At the bottom of the forestay will be a drum attached to a furling line. If you pull on the furling line the jib will wrap itself around the forestay, but the sail must be slack (out of the wind) for this to work. You will also need to ease the jib sheets as you go.

To unfurl the sail, you ease the furling line (under control) and pull on one of the jib sheets. The sail will then unwrap from the forestay and deploy. Don't force the furling line, it should turn easily under hand pressure, you shouldn't need to winch it.

Chapter 7:
Locating the Wind

Sailors depend on the wind to power their boats. Therefore, it is important to know in what direction it is coming from. Sailing is about harnessing the power of the wind, so as you can imagine, it's vital to first understand exactly which direction the wind is coming from.

Naturally, this can be done by feel, but there is a much easier way with the use of a telltale. The telltale, is a piece of yarn or fabric attached to a stay, any of several wires which hold a mast in place on a sailboat. They are used in pairs, on each side of the jib. Accordingly, there will be one telltale on the port stay and one on a starboard stay.

The wind on the water is shifty, changing often both in direction and in strength. This can cause difficulty for the beginner, as well as for the experienced sailor. Being aware of the wind's direction relative to your boat is of primary importance. Keep an eye on the tell-tales on your boat, as well as other indicators, such as flags on the shore, waves on the water, and the sail trim of nearby boats to give yourself an idea of what the wind is doing.

There are two rules when looking at the water for wind speed. If you see dark wrinkled patches of water that tends to indicate an increase in wind speed or a gust. On the other hand, if you see light glassy areas this tend to denote a decrease in wind speed or a lull.

Chapter 8:
Points of Sail

Sailing exploits wind and moves a boat through the water.

Wind on the sails can push – and even pull – the hull through the water. The wind direction determines how to position the sails to keep the boat moving forward. Sailors should know where the wind is coming from and the wind angle relative to their boat for sail-trim purposes.

Once you know the wind direction, you can trim the sails for the direction you want to go. In the simplest form of sailing, a boat and its sails can be pushed "downwind," with the wind coming over the stern. But keep in mind that if you sail downwind, you will need to work your way back upwind to return to your starting place.

In any event, you are going to want to get acquainted with the physics of sailing itself through the three basic Points of Sail which are:

- **Close Hauled**

- **Reaching (Close, Beam & Broad)**

- **Running**

As you can see, you cannot exactly sail directly into the wind, but you may sail 45 degrees into it. Anything over and you are in what is called the **No Go Zone** and are said to be **In Irons**.

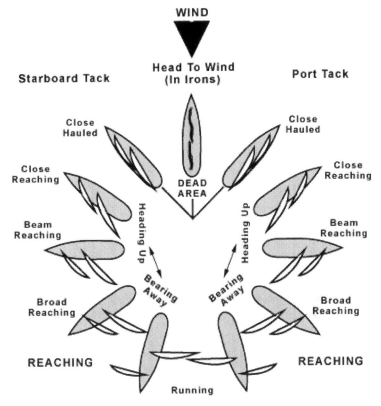

Points of sail are defined by the angle of the wind coming over the boat relative to the bow. Looking straight ahead at the bow would be looking towards the top of the clock or, 12 o'clock.

Close Hauled (also called "sailing to windward", "upwind sailing" or "beating") – sailing with the front of the boat as close as possible to the direction the wind is coming from without the sails luffing. The sail(s) are pulled in.

Reaching – sailing with the wind coming across the side of the boat. The sails are part way out.

- **Close reach**

  This is an upwind angle between close-hauled and a beam reach.

- **Beam reach**

  This is a course steered at right angles to the wind on either port or starboard tack.

- **Broad reach**

  The wind is coming from behind the boat at an angle. This represents a range of wind angles between beam reach and running downwind. The sails are eased out away from the boat, but not as much as on a run or dead run (downwind run).

Running (also called "downwind") – sailing with the wind coming from behind the boat. The sails are out.

If we want to use the wind, instead of an engine as our power source, we will do well to learn the effects of wind on the sails and how to most efficiently use this power freely supplied by nature.

Chapter 9:
Launching & Berthing

Launching:

If your sailboat or the one you are using is normally kept afloat, you will have to learn how to leave and return to the mooring, which is usually marked by a small pick-up buoy.

Picking up and leaving moorings is a relatively simple process - just as long as you take the tidal stream into account. Assess the effect of the tide by looking at yachts on swinging moorings or looking at the flow of water past objects fixed to the seabed.

On non-tidal water the boat will always point into the wind when left on a mooring, so that you can hoist the mainsail and jib before casting off. Therefore it would look something like this:

    1. Assess direction of wind.

    2. Prepare mooring line for slipping

    3. Hoist mainsail and jib.

    4. Back the jib, slip the mooring line and sail away.

Returning to Mooring Buoy/ Docking:

On the other hand, when returning to a mooring, first try to assess how your boat will end up lying at the mooring by seeing how other, similar boats are lying.

1. Assess direction of wind and tide.

2. Choose a close-hauled or close reach course to the buoy.

3. Prepare the yachts mooring line, leading it through the bow fairlead and stay ready with the boathook.

4. Let the jib fly.

5. Ease the mainsail to reduce speed and steer so that the boat stops with the buoy on the windward side of the bow.

6. Secure the mooring line.

7. Lower sails and de-rig the yacht.

Chapter 10:
Steering the Sailboat

Changing Directions:

Turning the sailboat away from the wind is to fall off or bear away. Turning into the wind is to head up or harden up. As the sailboat falls off the sails should be eased or let out. As the sailboat heads up the sails need to be trimmed or moved toward midline. When one changes the point-of-sail it is advantageous to change the position of the mainsail before or during the maneuver. For example, if you are going to change from a close reach to a broad reach, you should change the sail position before completing the turn or the wind will hit the sail at 90 degrees and may excessively heel the boat.

A sailboat can be steered by using the helm (tiller or Wheel), the sails , the angle of heel, and any combination of these. The beginning skipper should focus on properly using the helm.

Once aboard the vessel the helmsperson, the skipper, should always sit on the Windward side opposite the boom of the boat. In this position he will face the sail, and take hold of the tiller stick which is attached to the rudder used to control the direction of the vessel with the aft or near the back end of the boat.. The skipper will hold the mainsheet line attached to control the angle of attack.

To steer the vessel, the helmsman must move the tiller in the opposite direction from which he she wants to turn. The teller works by diverting water that flows around the rudderr; therefore the boat must be moving to turn efficiently. The tiller should be handled in a firm smooth manner. Sudden jerky movements disrupt the laminar flow of water across the surface of the rudder and may cause the tiller to act as a brake.

Chapter 11:
How Do I Stop the Boat?

There may be times out on the water when you either need to slow down or your out of control and you need to slam on the brakes. Perhaps you are coming in to your mooring? Perhaps you are practicing man-over-board exercises? Perhaps you need to avert another boat? Whatever the case, this is achieved by:

1. Steering you sailboat directly into the wind.

2. Easing the sheets and allowing the sails to luff.

There is yet another technique . If you are heading in with too speed around the mooring area you can slack the sail as in point 2 above, but then you can grab the sailboat boom and push it hard back against the wind. You can also use this back-wind technique when anchoring under sail too. Stop the boat, lower the anchor, and back-wind the mainsail. This will dig the boat anchor deep into the seabed--without an engine.

Chapter 12:
Tacking & Jibing

Changing Directions through the Wind

Sailing directly into the wind is impossible and sailing directly downwind is difficult and tricky. There are two basic maneuvers to change directions through the wind — Tacking (Coming About) and Jibing. We use one of these two maneuvers anytime the change in our course causes the wind to change from one side of the boat to the other. Both maneuvers will accomplish this objective. Tacking does so by taking the bow through the wind. On the other hand, Jibing does so by taking the stern through the wind. Which one you choose depends upon a number of factors. First is the direction you want to turn. Is it easier to turn to starboard (boat's right) or to port (boat's left) to steer to your new objective? If the closer turn takes the bow through the wind, it is generally better to tack. If it is closer to turn downwind and take the stern through the wind, then generally jibing is the desired maneuver. Other factors to consider are wind strength and proximity to obstructions such as shoals, wharfs or other boats. In stronger winds, jibing can be a more challenging maneuver, often intimidating less experienced sailors as well as subjecting the boat and its equipment to serious stress due to the rapid shift of the wind force from one side to another. If conditions warrant we'll probably do what we call a "Chicken Jibe" which is heading up and tacking around the long way.

Tacking: In this maneuver, the bow of the boat goes through the wind as one changes from a close-hauled point-of-sail on one tack (direction) to a close hauled point-of-sail on the other direction. Only the jib needs to be adjusted, the working sheet of the jib is changed and the new working sheet is placed on a winch. The mainsail is left alone and will by itself often assume the correct position. In this manner, the sailboat can zigzag a course almost against the wind.

Commands

- Skipper - Ready about!

- Crew - Ready!

- Skipper - Helm's Alee!

- Skipper - Trim to course!

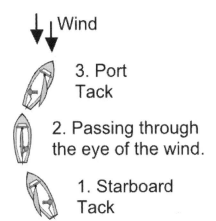

Jibing: In this maneuver, the stern of the boat goes through the wind as one changes from a broad reach on one tack (direction) to a broad reach in the other tack (direction). Both the jib and mainsail will need adjusting. The mainsail is first centered, the turn made and the mainsail is then let out. Be sure the mainsheet is free to run! The jib's working sheet is changed and the new working sheet is placed on a winch.

Commands

- Skipper - Prepare to jibe!

- Crew - Ready!

- Skipper - Center the mainsail!

- Crew - Centered!

- Skipper - Jibe Ho!

- Skipper - Trim to course!

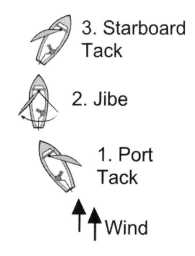

3. Starboard Tack

2. Jibe

1. Port Tack

Wind

Chapter 13:
Right of Way for Sailboats

Collisions occur between boats more often than you might think, usually because one or both captains did not know or were not applying the Rules of the Road. Whenever two boats come close to each other, the rules designate one as the stand-on vessel and the other as the give-way vessel.

<u>Rules of the Road</u>

A sailboat will always give way to -

- A disabled vessel or a vessel not under command;

- Vessels restricted in their ability to maneuver;

- A vessel restricted by draft;

- A vessel engaged in fishing .

When one sailboat meets another -

- The boat on a port tack shall give way to one on a starboard tack.

- If on the same tack, the windward boat shall give way to a leeward boat when on the same tack.

- A boat that is overtaking shall give way to a boat ahead, regardless to the type of vessels or tack.

- A boat coming about (tacking) or jibing shall give way to a boat on a steady heading. Thus, if your vessel is the stand-on vessel you are required not to turn or alter course. If the stand-on vessel does alter course it must be to avoid a collision. If your vessel is the give-way vessel you must turn away from the stand-on vessel to avoid a collision.

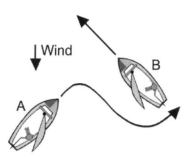

Sailboat vs. Powerboat

Remember that a sailboat running an engine, even if sails are up, is legally categorized as a powerboat. In a congested area it is best not to run the engine with sails still up, because captains of other boats may not be aware of your engine running and may assume you are operating under sailing rules.

The Rules are simple when a sailboat and a small recreational powerboat meet:

- In most situations the sailing boat is the stand-on vessel and the powerboat must give way.

- If the sailboat is overtaking a powerboat, the powerboat is the stand-on vessel and the sailboat must give way.

- As a rule of thumb, any boat with more maneuverability must give way to any boat with less maneuverability.

Chapter 14:
Safety First

When you sail it is important to know some things about safety. To begin with you should know how to swim, wear a PFD and check the weather. Needless to say,on sunny days don't forget the sunscreen on cold says don't forget your cold weather gear. In the main, you should employ common sense. Remember accidents happen when you least expect them.

For starters, if you are new to sailing, the boom may show itself to be one of the most dangerous things on a boat as it swings over the hull and cockpit during maneuvers such as the Tack and the Jibe. Just make sure you stay clear. They don't call it a boom for nothing. Moreover, moving about a boat can also be dangerous. There are lots of things to bump into and a boat might lurch unexpectedly. The rule for moving about a boat is: one hand for you and one for the boat. Always hold onto something when moving around.

Sailboat safety involves a wide range of activities and the use of important safety gear and equipment. As a rule of thumb, you should be aware of what has come to be known as the 7 F's of safety:

- **Fire** – what firefighting equipment is on board? Where are the extinguishers? How do you turn off the gas for the stove? (Never smoke inside a cabin on a yacht – it's a recipe for disaster)

- **Flooding** – what happens if the boat is full of water? How do you pump it out? Where is the bucket to bail water out if the pump fails? Nothing shifts water faster than a wet crewman with a bucket!

- **Flotation devices** – okay, so the bucket didn't work. What now? Where are the life jackets, life rings and other floatation devices? Do you have a life raft? How does it work?

- **First aid** – what happens when the skipper cuts his finger opening the Chardonnay? Where do you keep the aspirin and alka-seltzer for hangovers? Where are the seasick pills?

- **Flashlight** – navigating at night requires a flashlight. It can also be used for signalling other boats or signalling for help. You should have at least one if not two on board.

- **Flares** – if you need to signal for help you might have to use a flare. Flares come in two basic types, smoke and signal. Signal flares give off intense heat and light. Smoke flares give off smoke and are mainly used to signal aircraft or other vessels of your precise location.

Signal flares come in two colors – red and white. Red flares are known as 'distress' flares because they are used when you want to be rescued. White flares are known as 'ship scarers' because they are used to alert other ships to your presence.

Flares are only useful if you can see someone who might rescue you. They won't attract someone from beyond visual range. So, don't waste them!

After use throw the flare overboard! Flares are hot enough to burn straight through a boat!

- **Phone** – Well, the last F is actually a P, but I hope you won't hold that against me. I use the phone to represent a Radio. Ensue that you have a proper Radio in the event you would need to mayday for help.

Chapter 15:
Man Overboard Drills

Clearly, one of the most significant things anyone can learn in the sailing world is how to efficiently and quickly return to someone who has fallen overboard. If you know how to perform these maneuvers you will be a more confident and skilled sailor.

I think it is important to know at least two different Man Overboard maneuvers. Naturally, to practice use a practice buoy to recover. In your own boat, one of these will probably work better than another.

The Figure Eight Maneuver

The **figure eight method** is a classic approach often taught to beginning sailors on smaller vessels. Since it does not require a jibe, this method eliminates the potential danger of an uncontrolled boom flying across the cockpit and banging somebody in the head or damaging the rigging. It looks like this:

1. Regardless of which point of sail you are on when a crewmember falls overboard, the figure eight method starts with yelling "Man overboard," throwing flotation devices and appointing a spotter.

2. The helmsman should immediately either head up or bear away (depending on which point of sail the boat is on) to a beam reach.

3. Sail six to eight boat lengths on a beam reach.

4. Tack and immediately bear away from the wind to a broad reach, but only briefly until you cross your wake.

5. Head up to a close reach, ease the sheets and pick the victim up on the leeward side with speed between 1 and 2 knots and sails luffing.

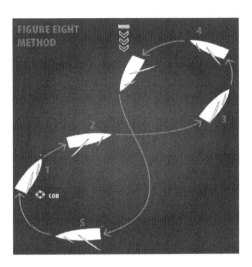

Quick-Stop Maneuver

The first is the **Quick-Stop Maneuver**. This technique can work very well and the boat always remains close to the victim. This does require a jibe but is done with control as the main sheet is brought in. It is executed as follows:

1. Shout "Man overboard," throw flotation devices overboard and appoint a spotter.

2. The helmsman points the boat directly into the wind and comes to a stop or near stop.

3. Leaving the sheets alone, backwind the jib or genoa and tack.

4. Sail downwind in a circle around the person in the water.

5. Release the jib or genoa sheet and jibe the boat.

6. Head back toward the victim on a close reach with sails luffing and pick them up on the leeward side. Variations of this method include furling or dropping the forward sail when heading downwind or approaching the victim close hauled or head to wind rather than on a close reach.

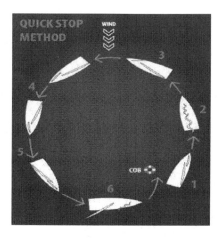

Chapter 16:
Capsizing and Righting

Although this book predominantly concerns itself with basic keelboats, you may find yourself sailing dinghies such as the Sailfish or Club240 or bigger. These boats do not have weighted keels. Instead, they have retractable centerboards. In any event, learning to right a capsized dinghy should be part of learning to sail.

If you sail long enough you will capsize. Capsizing should not be considered as a serious accident. It can happen to the best of sailors. It should, however, be practiced. When practicing, follow the steps listed below. In light air with calm water it is possible for one light person to right the boat, but you may be surprised when it takes at least two to accomplish the same job in heavy air.

Steps to righting a capsized Dinghy:

1. Make sure everyone is safe – Yell, "Is everyone ok?" Everyone should grab onto the boat for safety. If someone is trapped under the main, they should move or be guided to the leech of the main. If someone is injured they may need assistance in getting to the bottom-side of the boat where they can hold on (perhaps even to the rudder) while the others right the boat.

2. Swim to the centerboard – At least one person should swim as quickly as possible to the bottom-side of the boat and grab the centerboard to help prevent the boat from turning turtle. Avoid climbing from inside the

boat over the gunwale to the centerboard; this will cause the boat to turn turtle.

3. Wear PFDs – Everyone should already be wearing a PFD, but if anyone is not, they need to put it on now.

4. Retrieve floating items – At this point, if you can swim well enough, you can retrieve any floating items before they get too far from the boat.

5. Prepare boat – If the spinnaker is up, it should be lowered before righting the boat. Make sure the main sheet, jib sheets, and vang are uncleated.

6. Bow heading into the wind – Before righting the boat, make sure the bow is heading somewhat into the wind. If it is not, one person can go to the bow and swim it into the wind. Having the bow pointing somewhat into the wind will allow the boat to point into irons as it is righting. This lessens the chance of the boat re-capsizing.

7. Right the boat – At least one person climbs onto the centerboard and, if possible, reaches up for the rail for more leverage. The boat should slowly right. If it does not, a second person may be needed on the centerboard. Bring the boat up slowly to give the boat time to turn into the wind.

8. Don't re-capsize the boat – As the boat comes up fall into the water so you do not capsize the boat on top of you. Keep holding onto the rail so the boat does not drift away.

9. Get back in – The boat will be full of water when it is righted. The lightest or most agile person should climb

into the boat first. Climb into the boat near the transom where the boat is generally closest to the waterline. Once one person is in the boat they can assist the others. It may be that only two people can get into the boat until enough water is bailed to allow the third person to climb in. 1

10. Bail and sail – Bail most of the water out of the boat before sailing. The boat may now be sailed fast enough on a reach with the bailiers open to remove the remaining water.

11. Beware of hypothermia – If anyone is feeling at all cold, sail back in so they can change into dry clothes.

A turtled boat is when the boat is upside down with the mast pointing into the water. The following steps can be used to get a turtled boat to be a capsized boat

1. Get the centerboard exposed – If the centerboard is showing, grab it and, if possible, pull it out to its full length.

2. Unturtle the boat – By holding onto the centerboard and standing on the underside off the rail, it may be possible to get the boat to the capsized position.

3. Using a line – If the preceeding does not work a line will have to be tied to the boat. One end of the line is tied to the boat's forward grating or to the shroud and the other end of the line is tied to the boat's aft grating to form a loop or bridle which can be thrown over the bottom of the boat. A rigged spinnaker sheet, if available, may work as a bridle.

4. Unturtle the boat – One or two people need to reach for the bridle line to climb onto the bottom of the boat. They stand on the underside of the rail and pull on the bridle or put the bridle around their back. By leaning back the turtled boat can be brought to the capsized position. The boat will turn very slowly.

5. Push the centerboard back down – In a turtled boat, the centerboard has likely fallen to the wrong side of the boat. If this has happened, push the centerboard back into place.

6. Right the boat – At this point, follow the directions above for righting a capsized boat.

Conclusion

You have taken in a large amount of information in these chapters.

I had a lot of goals when I set out to write this book, but the most important of these was to shed light sailing and to get you out on the water.

Whether you have never been sailing or would like to know enough to be helpful on your friend's boat or plan to get your own boat this book has something for you.

I hope you have found this book to be a useful tool in gaining a better understanding of just what sailing is all about.

I have taken you through a lot about sailing and how it all works. You know why the boat moves through the water, you have learned how to launch and return to your mooring, you know about the different points of sail and you have even learned what to do when the skipper says: "**Prepare to Come About**"!

Thank you for the time you took to read this book.

Happy Sailing!

Glossary

Abeam - Off to the side of a vessel at right angles to the boat's centerline.

Aboard- On or in the boat

Anchor- A device used to hold a boat to the sea bottom

Aft- At, near or towards the stern.

Apparent Wind- The wind that flows over a moving boat, which is a result of the "true wind" affected by the movement of the boat.

Appendage- An underwater fin such as a centerboard dagger board, t\leeboard or rudder.

Astern- Behind the boat

Backing- Pushing out a sail so that the wind fills it from the opposite side. Used to slow a boat or turn the bow away away from the wind when in irons; back winding – a sail backwinds with the wind funneling on the wrong side.

Bailer- A device used to remove water from the boat. A bailer is required equipment for a Sabot.

Batten- Thin fiberglass or wood slats that are inserted in the leech (outside) of the sail for added support.

Beam- Maximum width of a boat;

Beam reach- sailing at approximately 90 degrees to the wind with the wind coming from abeam and the sails eased about half way.

Beat- Advance to windward on alternate tacks; beating – to sail to windward, close-hauled, tacking to make way to windward.

Bitter end- End of a line.

Block- A pulley that is encased in its own housing. A block will help to add purchase when pulling on a line. It is important to use the correct size line with the blocks on your boat.

Bolt rope- Sewn around luff and foot of sails to give added strength to sail where it attaches to mast or boom.

Boom- Horizontal spar that supports the foot (bottom) of the sail. Named for the sound it makes when it hits someone's head.

Boom Vang- A line that runs from the boom to the base of the mast. The vang helps keep the boom down and tighten the back (leech) of the sail.

Bow-The forward part of a boat, the pointy end.

Bow Line- Also known as a painter. The bow line is used to tie the boat to the dock or to a tow line. Minimum 10 foot bowline is required equipment. Best if at least ¼" in diameter.

Broad Reach- Sailing with the wind coming over the rear corner of the boat (quarter), or with the bow approximately 120-160 degrees from the source (eye) of the wind.

By-the-lee- Running with the wind on the same side as the boom, increasing the possibility of an accidental jibe.

Burgee-A flag, often triangular, that serves as the unique emblem for each yacht club.

Capsize- A boat turned over on its side or upside down (turtled).

Cast off- To untie a line and let it go, or remove a line from a cleat and let it go.

Catamaran- A boat with two parallel hulls.

Centerboard- A thin, wide blade going down through the bottom of the hull in the center of the boat. This blade helps to keep the boat from going sideways in the water. It serves the same purpose as a leeboard or a dagger board.

Center of Effort- Center of sail area, the focal point of the forces generated by the sail area.

Clea- A fitting where a line can be secured.

Clew- The aft lower corner of the sail is the clew. It is where the foot and the leech of the sail meet.

Close-hauled- Sailing as close to the wind as possible.

Close reach- Sailing with the wind forward of the beam, or with the bow approximately 60 degrees from the eye of the wind.

Clove Hitch- Similar to two half hitch knot. Most often used to hang fenders over side of boat for protection. Course The direction a boat is steered to reach a destination; or the compass heading; or the angle a boat is sailing relative to the wind. Crew The people who help the helmsperson sail a boat.

Cockpit- Open part of boat.

Cunningham- A control line used to tension the forward edge (luff) of a sail, similar to a downhaul.

Dagger board-Foil raised and lowered vertically used to reduce leeway, different from centerboard which is pivoted instead of raised.

Dinghy- An open boat, or one partially decked over without a cabin.

Dolly- A lightweight trailer that is used to move boats from their storage rack to the launch dock.

Ease- To slack a line or sail, ie. To "sheet" out.

Eye of the Wind- From the source of the wind; directly into the direction from which the wind is blowing from, the no-sailzone.

Fairlead Block- Fitting used to change the direction of a running line such a jib sheet.

Feathering- Sailing upwind so close to the wind that the forward edge of the sail is stalling or luffing, slightly thus reducing the power generated by the sail and the angle of heel without stalling completely. Fenders Cushions to reduce the chafe between a boat and the dock or other boats

Fiberglass- Most modern boats are made of fiberglass. It is a woven material impregnated with a liquid resin that is very stiff when the resin dries.

Figure 8 knot- Stopper knot in the shape of an "8" used for the end of a line to prevent it from passing through a fairlead or eye.

Fleet- For racing purposes, sailors are grouped in fleets according to experience.

Foot- The bottom edge of the sail between the tack (front corner) and the clew (back corner).

Forestay- Forward support of mast, usually wire lead from bow to mast, part of the standing rigging. Give way The boat which must alter course to avoid another boat, the burdened boat in the Rules of the Road Gooseneck A hinged fitting on the mast that connects the mast to the boom.

Grommet- A metal ring in a sail that allows lines to be connected through or to the sail. Both the clew and the tack have grommets.

Gudgeon- A "U" shaped fitting on the back of a boat used to connect the rudder to the hull. Most sailing dinghies have two gudgeons.

Halyards- Lines that are attached to the head of a sail and used to hoist sails up the mast. Head The top of the sail.

Header- A wind direction change "shift" that brings the wind closer to the bow. Heading The direction the boat is travelling at any given moment.

Head Up- Turn the bow of the boat toward the wind.

Heel- To lean a boat over, generally away from the wind.

Helm 1) the tiller; 2) the tendency of a boat to turn toward the wind (weather helm) or away from the wind (lee helm) Helmsperson The person who steers a boat, ie. skipper

Hiking Out- The action of hanging over the side of the boat in order to keep the boat flat on the water.

Hiking Boots- Special boots made of thick rubber that protect and support a sailor's ankles when using the hiking strap to hike out.

Hiking Strap- A strap, usually stiff, sometimes padded for comfort, attached to the bottom of the cockpit under which a sailor places his/her feet in order to hold the sailor in the boat while hiking out.

Hull- The actual body of the boat.

In irons- A boat head to wind with all sails luffing and no maneuverability.

Inspection Port- A hole in the hull of the boat that allows the skipper to reach inside the hull to make repairs, or sponge out water.

Jib- The front sail on boats with two or more sails. It is small and triangular in shape.

Jibe (Gybe)- Turning the boat away from the wind so the stern passes through the wind and the sail(s) switches sides..

Lee- The area sheltered from the wind, downwind; leeward (pronounced loo-ward) – the direction away from the wind, the side of the boat opposite the windward side.

Leech- The aft edge of the sail. The leech connects the head and the clew of the sail.

Life jacket- A jacket type device that provides flotation when sailors are in the water

Luff or Luffing- 1) The forward edge of the sail nearest the mast, between the tack and the head of the sail; 2) when a sail is waving back and forth as the sail is "eased" out too much or the boat is heading into the wind, the sail is said to be luffing, like a flag flying in the breeze. 3) when the boat turns its bow toward the wind the boat is said to be luffing.

Mainsheet- The line attached to the boom that controls the Mainsail in and out.

Mast- The vertical spar that supports the sail.

Mast blocks- Small pieces of wood or plastic used to support the mast in a forward or aft position.

Mast Tube- A tube on a Sabot that the mast fits into and supports the mast.

Outhaul- A line attached to the clew of the mainsail and used to stretch the sail out along the boom. The outhaul controls the "depth" of the sail.

Paddle- A small board or device used to move the boat in case of emergency or lack of wind. Paddle is required equipment on many small boats.

Pintles- The pins on the rudder that are inserted into the gudgeons on the transom of the boat to connect the rudder to the hull.

Planing- When a boat accelerates enough to break loose from its bow wave and ride on top of the water.

Port- Refers to the left side of the boat as well as to which tack a boat is on. If a boat is on "port tack" the wind is coming over the left side of the boat.

Ratchet Block- These are special blocks that rotate in only one direction. They grip the line passing through the ratchet block, relieving some of the "pull" on that line.

Reach Sail- with the wind over the side. i.e A Beam reach is the wind approx. 90 degrees from the bow, broad reach 130-170 degrees from the bow, or close reach with the wind 55-80 from the bow.

Rudder- The movable, underwater blade on the transom of the boat used for steering.

Run- Sail downwind, with the wind aft or nearly so, ie. Sailing with the wind.

Sail- The part of the boat's equipment which is usually made from cloth and which is attached to the mast and is the boat's primary reason for movement.

Sea breeze- Wind from the ocean caused by warm air rising over the land and the cool ocean wind replacing it.

Shackle- A U shaped metal ring with a pin to close the "U". It is used to connect objects together, such as connecting the jib halyard to the head (top) of the jib.

Sheets- All lines on a boat which are used to control the in and out motion of sail.

S-Hook- A stainless steel "S" shaped hook used on the end of many control lines that allows for quick hook up and disconnect.

Shrouds- Wires that hold the mast to the sides of the boat and support the power of the sails. Part of the standing rigging.

Skipper- The person in charge of the boat, usually the person steering the boat.

Stand on- To hold course, the privileged boat in the Rules of the Road.

Starboard- Refers to the right side of the boat. A boat is on a "starboard tack" when the wind is on its starboard side (coming over the right side of the boat).

Stern- Aft (back) end of a boat.

Stopper knot- A knot on the end of a line to prevent it from passing through a block, like the Figure 8 knot.

Tack- 1) If a boat's bow passes through the eye of the wind, then it is said to be tacking. 2) The direction the boat is sailing (see starboard and port). 3) The lower front corner of the sail where the luff and the foot of the sail meet.

Telltales- Small lengths of lightweight material attached to the sail near the luff or batten pockets of main sail to indicate the airflow over the sail.

Thwart- A structural board in the center of a Sabot. Juniors should sit next to the thwart when sailing.

Tiller- The long piece of wood that is connected to the top of the rudder. It changes the boat's direction when moved from side to side.

Transom- The very back edge of the boat is called the transom. It is where the name of the boat is often painted.

Traveler- A line or track that controls sideways movement of the boom and mainsail.

Trim- 1)Pulling or "sheeting" in a sail. 2)Fore and aft balance of a boat or 3)can be used to refer to the adjustment of sails to take the best advantage of the wind.

True wind- The speed and direction of the wind felt by a stationary object.

Turtle, turn turtle- When a vessel is capsized and completely inverted so that its hull is above the water and its mast is submerged.

US SAILING- The United States Sailing Association. All sailors should belong to this organization. US Sailing sponsors all Junior National Sailing Championship events.

Weather- Toward the wind.

Windward- The general direction the wind is coming from.

Wing and wing- Running before the wind with the main sail and jib on opposite sides of the boat

81466389R00035

Made in the USA
San Bernardino, CA
07 July 2018